Introduction

Deck the Halls & Raid the Stash!

In this exciting pattern book, we've got more than 20 ornaments to keep those idle hands busy all season long as you happily knit the hours away, creating handmade ornaments for your very own tree and as treasured gifts for friends and family.

Making these ornaments is easy on the wallet too. Christmas ornaments are small, which means you don't need to invest vast amounts of time or money in making them. Also, these charming projects are made using a variety of yarn weights so you can easily find your gauge and conveniently use whatever yarns you have on hand.

If you're up for learning some new techniques, then you are in luck too. In *Deck the Halls*, you'll discover openwork techniques, knitting with beads, knitting in the round, stranded colorwork, shaping with short rows and drop stitch. You'll also be delighted by the range of familiar friends—we've got Jolly Old St. Nick of course, Donner the reindeer, Elfie the Christmas elf and Agnes the lamb to name just a few.

Let's pick up our needles and yarn and make some Christmas magic!

Table of Contents

Wish Upon A Star, *page 21*

Snowdie

Make your own snowman and stay toasty warm inside by the fire—no mittens required!

Design by Lena Skvagerson for Annie's Signature Designs

Skill Level

 INTERMEDIATE

Finished Measurement

Approx 4 inches tall

Materials

- Premier Yarns Deborah Norville Everyday Soft Worsted (worsted weight; 100% acrylic; 203 yds/100g per skein): 1 skein cream #1002 (A) **4 MEDIUM**
- Premier Yarns Deborah Norville Serenity Sock Solids (fingering weight; 50% wool/25% nylon/ 25% rayon; 230 yds/50g per skein): 1 skein red #5003 (B) **1 SUPER FINE**
- Fingering weight yarn: Small amounts each black (C) and orange/rust (D)
- Size 2 (2.75mm) knitting needles
- Size 8 (5mm) double-point needles (set of 4) or size needed to obtain gauge
- Small crochet hook (for attaching fringe)
- Fiberfill

Gauge

18 sts and 24 rnds = 4 inches/10cm in St st using larger needles and A.

Exact gauge is not critical for this project.

Special Technique

4-St I-Cord: Cast on 4 sts; do not turn. *Slip sts back to LH needle, k4, do not turn; rep from * until cord is desired length. Bind off.

Pattern Notes

Snowman is worked in the round from bottom up.

One skein of A will yield approximately 3 ornaments.

Scarf can be made with color of choice.

Body

With larger needles and A, cast on 6 sts. Distribute sts evenly on 3 dpns; mark beg of rnd and join, being careful not to twist.

Rnd 1: Knit.

Rnd 2: [Yo, k1] 6 times—12 sts.

Rnds 3, 5, 7 and 9: Knit, working yo's tbl.

Rnd 4: [Yo, k2] 6 times—18 sts.

Rnd 6: [Yo, k3] 6 times—24 sts.

Rnd 8: [Yo, k4] 6 times—30 sts.

Rnds 10–16: Knit.

Rnd 17: K2tog around—15 sts.

Rnd 18: Knit.

Head

Rnd 1: [Yo, k2, yo, k3] 3 times—21 sts.

Rnds 2–10: Knit, working yo's tbl on Rnd 2.

Stuff body and head with fiberfill.

K2tog around until 6 sts rem.

Cut yarn, leaving a 5-inch tail.

Using tapestry needle, thread tail through rem sts, and pull tight.

Finishing

Note: *Refer to photo for embellishments.*

Using tapestry needle, thread cast-on tail through cast-on sts, and pull tight.

Weave in ends.

Scarf

With smaller needles and B, cast on 60 sts.

Knit 8 rows.

Bind off.

Fringe

Cut 16 3-inch strands of B. *Fold 1 strand in half. With RS of scarf facing and beg at corner of 1 edge, use crochet hook to draw folded end from RS to WS. Pull loose ends through folded section. Draw knot up firmly. Rep from *, placing 8 evenly spaced fringes along each short edge. Trim even.

Tie scarf around snowman's neck.

Embroidery

Buttons: With C, embroider 3 X's down center front of body, using cross stitches 1 knit st wide and 2 rows high and leaving 1 row between each X.

Eyes: With C, embroider 2 small X's on face, using small cross sts 1 knit st wide and 1 row high.

Carrot Nose

With smaller needles and D, work 4 rnds I-Cord, do not turn.

Next rnd: K1, k2tog, k1; do not turn—3 sts.

Knit 1 rnd; do not turn; k3tog—1 st.

Cut yarn, and fasten off last st.

Weave in tail.

Sew cast-on edge to snowman's face.

Twisted-Cord Hanger

Cut 30-inch strand of A. Fold in half and secure folded end to a stationary object. Twist yarn until it begins to double back on itself. Fold in half again with both ends tog and allow to twist on itself. Thread cord through top of head. Tie ends tog in a knot; trim ends close to knot. Rotate cord so that knot is inside head ●

Donner

With just bits of stash yarns, why not give some new techniques a try and make the cutest little reindeer? You have nothing to lose and new skills to gain!

Design by Lena Skvagerson for Annie's Signature Designs

Skill Level

■■■◻ EXPERIENCED

Finished Measurements

Length: Approx 5¾ inches

Height: 4 inches

Materials

- Premier Yarns Deborah Norville Serenity Sock Solids (fingering weight; 50% wool/25% nylon/25% rayon; 230 yds/50g per skein): 1 skein each deep brown #5006 (A), soft white #5001 (B) and red #5003 (C)

  1 SUPER FINE

- Fingering weight yarn: Small amount black for eyes
- Size 2 (2.75mm) double-point needles (set of 4) or size needed to obtain gauge
- Fiberfill

Gauge

32 sts and 42 rnds = 4 inches/10cm in St st.

To save time, take time to check gauge.

Special Technique

6-St I-Cord: With dpns, cast on 6 sts. *Do not turn, slide sts to other end of dpn, pull yarn taut across back, k6; rep from * until cord is desired length. Bind off.

Pattern Notes

Legs, body and head are worked in the round, stuffed and then sewn together.

One skein of A will yield approximately 2 ornaments.

Leg

Make 4

With A, cast on 6 sts and divide on 3 dpns. Mark beg of rnd and join, being careful not to twist sts.

Rnd 1: [K1, yo, k1] 3 times—9 sts.

Rnd 2: [Yo, k3] 3 times, working yo's from Rnd 1 tbl to twist—12 sts.

Rnd 3: Knit, working yo's tbl.

Rnd 4: Purl.

Rnd 5: Knit.

Rnd 6: [K2tog, k2] 3 times—9 sts.

Stuff leg with a little fiberfill as you go.

Rnds 7–9: With B, knit. Cut B.

Rnds 10–25: With A, knit.

Bind off.

Cut A, leaving a 6-inch tail for sewing leg to body.

Body

Note: Body is worked from back to front.

With A, cast on 6 sts and divide on 3 dpns. Mark beg of rnd and join, being careful not to twist sts.

Rnd 1: [K1, yo] 6 times—12 sts.

Rnds 2, 4, 6 and 8: Knit, working yo's tbl.

Rnd 3: [K2, yo] 6 times—18 sts.

Rnd 5: [K3, yo] 6 times—24 sts.

Rnd 7: [K4, yo] 6 times—30 sts.

Knit 20 rnds.

Chest

Note: Beg of rnd is under the stomach.

Work short rows as follows:

Row 1 (RS): K14, turn.

Row 2 (WS): P28, turn.

Row 3: K27, turn.

Row 4: P26, turn.

Row 5: K25, turn.

Row 6: P24, turn.

Row 7: K23, turn.

Row 8: P22, turn.

Next rnd: K22, [pick up and knit 1 st before next st on LH needle, then slip new st to LH needle; k2tog (new st and next st)] 4 times, (center neck), k1, [pick up and knit 1 st before next st on LH needle, then slip new st to LH needle; k2tog (new st and next st)] 4 times, k10—30 sts.

Shape Neck

Rnd 1: [K3, k2tog] 6 times—24 sts.

Rnd 2: [K2, k2tog] 6 times—18 sts.

Rnd 3: [K1, k2tog] 6 times—12 sts.

Bind off.

Cut yarn, leaving an 8-inch tail for sewing head to neck.

Stuff with fiberfill.

Head

Note: Head is worked from nose to back of head. The 13 sts between yo's established on Rnds 6–12 are top of head.

With B, cast on 6 sts and divide on 3 dpns. Mark beg of rnd and join, being careful not to twist sts.

Rnd 1: Knit.

Rnd 2: [Yo, k1] 6 times—12 sts.

Rnd 3 and all odd-numbered rnds: Knit around, working all yo's of previous rnd tbl.

Rnd 4: [Yo, k2] 6 times—18 sts.

After Rnd 5, cut B and join A.

Rnd 6: K1, yo, k5, yo, k12—20 sts.

Rnd 8: K1, yo, k7, yo, k12—22 sts.

Rnd 10: K1, yo, k9, yo, k12—24 sts.

Rnd 12: K1, yo, k11, yo, k12—26 sts.

Knit 13 rnds.

Dec rnd: K2tog around—13 sts.

Stuff with fiberfill.

Knit 1 rnd.

Last rnd: [K2tog] 6 times, k1—7 sts.

Cut yarn, leaving a 5-inch tail.

Using tapestry needle, thread tail through rem sts, and pull tight.

Weave in ends.

Tail

With A, cast on 6 sts, leaving a 6-inch tail for sewing tail to body

Work I-Cord for 6 rnds; after last rnd, do not turn, slide sts.

Rnd 7: K1, [k2tog] twice, k1; do not turn, slide sts—4 sts.

Rnd 8: [K2tog] twice—2 sts.

Cut yarn, leaving a 5-inch tail.

Using tapestry needle, thread tail through rem sts, and pull tight.

Weave in end.

Antler
Make 2

With A, cast on 9 sts.

Rows 1 and 2: Knit.

Row 3: Bind off 4 sts, knit to end—5 sts.

Row 4: Bind off 3 sts, k2.

Rows 5 and 6: K2.

Bind off.

Weave in ends.

Scarf

With C, cast on 60 sts.

Knit 4 rows.

Bind off.

Weave in ends.

Assembly

Note: Refer to photo while assembling.

Using tail from neck, sew head to body, making sure to center the 13 sts that were established between incs (on Rnds 6–12) at top of head.

Using tails, sew legs to body.

Using cast-on tail, sew tail to back of body.

Sew antlers to head.

With black yarn, embroider eyes on head.

Tie scarf around the neck; tack to secure.

Twisted-Cord Hanger

Cut 30-inch strand of A. Fold in half and secure folded end to a stationary object. Twist yarn until it begins to double back on itself. Fold in half again with both ends tog and allow to twist on itself. Thread cord through top of back. Tie ends tog in a knot; trim ends close to knot. Rotate cord so that knot ends up inside body. ●

Elfie

You'll enjoy seeing this little guy spring to life on your needles. The kiddies will think he's pretty cool too!

Design by Lena Skvagerson
for Annie's Signature Designs

Skill Level

 INTERMEDIATE

Finished Measurement

Approx 6 inches tall

Materials

- Premier Yarns Deborah Norville Serenity Sock Solids (fingering weight; 50% wool/ 25% nylon/ 25% rayon; 230 yds/50g per skein): 1 skein each soft white #5001 (A), red #5003 (B), woodsy green #5007 (C) and deep brown #5006 (D)
- Fingering weight yarn: 1 yd each beige (E) and black (F)
- Size 2 (2.75mm) double-point needles (set of 5) or size needed to obtain gauge
- Stitch markers
- Stitch holders (optional)
- Fiberfill

SUPER FINE 1

Gauge

32 sts and 42 rnds = 4 inches/10cm in St st.

To save time, take time to check gauge.

Special Abbreviation

Make 1 (M1): Insert LH needle from front to back under horizontal strand between last st worked and next st on LH needle; knit through back of resulting loop.

Pattern Notes

Ornament is made in 1 piece. Legs and arms are worked separately in the round and stuffed, then incorporated into the body; piece ends at top of head and hat.

Weave in yarn tails at color changes as you go.

Yarn amounts listed will yield approximately 11 ornaments.

Elf

Arm
Make 2

With E and leaving a 5-inch tail, cast on 4 sts.

Row 1: Kfb in each st across, do not turn—8 sts.

Distribute to 4 dpns. Mark beg of rnd and join, being careful not to twist sts.

Rnd 2: [K1, kfb] 4 times—12 sts.

Rnd 3: Knit.

Change to A.

Rnd 4: [K2, k2tog] 3 times—9 sts.

Rnds 5 and 6: Purl.

Change to C.

Rnds 7–20: Knit.

Last rnd: Bind off 2 sts, knit to end—7 sts.

Use cast-on tail to close up cast-on opening.

Stuff arm with fiberfill.

Put sts on st holder or waste yarn.

Left Leg

With C and leaving a 5-inch tail, cast on 4 sts.

Row 1: Kfb in each st across, do not turn—8 sts.

Distribute to 4 dpns. Mark beg of rnd and join, being careful not to twist sts.

Rnd 2: [K1, kfb] 4 times—12 sts.

Rnd 3: Kfb, k10, kfb—14 sts.

Rnds 4–6: Knit.

Rnd 7: K4, [k2tog] 3 times, k4; cut C—11 sts.

With A, knit 2 rnds; cut A.

With B, knit 10 rnds.

Last rnd: K7, bind off 2 sts—9 sts rem.

Use cast-on tail to close up cast-on opening.

Stuff leg with fiberfill.

Beg at bound-off opening, transfer sts to waste yarn.

Right Leg

Work as for left leg to last rnd.

Last rnd: K2, bind off 2 sts, knit to end of rnd, slip marker, k2—9 sts rem.

Close up cast-on opening and stuff leg with fiberfill.

Body

Transfer left leg sts to a dpn.

With B, k9 from left leg, then k9 from right leg; pm for beg of rnd (middle back)—18 sts.

Rnd 1: Kfb in each st around—36 sts.

Rnd 2: Knit.

Rnd 3: *K3, kfb; rep from * around; cut B—45 sts.

Rnd 4: With A, knit.

Rnds 5 and 6: Purl. Cut A.

Rnd 7: With C, *k3, k2tog; rep from * around—36 sts.

Rnds 8–14: Knit; do not cut C.

Rnd 15: With D, knit.

Rnds 16 and 17: Purl; cut D.

Rnd 18: With C, *k4, k2tog; rep from * around—30 sts.

Rnds 19–23: Knit.

Rnd 24: K7, bind off 2, knit to last 9 sts, bind off 2, knit to end. Body sts are now divided as follows: 7 sts, 12 sts, 7 sts.

Shoulders

Transfer arm sts to 2 spare dpns.

Rnd 1: K7 body sts, k7 sts from first arm, k12 body sts, k7 sts from 2nd arm, k7 body sts—40 sts.

Rnd 2: K2tog round—20 sts.

Rnd 3: Knit. Cut C.

Sew openings under the arms and between the legs closed.

Stuff body with fiberfill.

Rnd 4: With B, knit.

Rnds 5 and 6: Purl. Cut B.

Head

Change to A and work short rows as follows:

Row 1 (RS): *K9, M1, k2, M1, k7, turn—2 sts inc.

Row 2 (WS): Sl 1, p7, M1, p2, M1, p8, turn—2 sts inc.

Row 3: Sl 1, k8, M1, k2, M1, k7, turn—2 sts inc.

Row 4: Sl 1, p17, turn.

Row 5: Sl 1, k5, ssk, k2, k2tog, k4, turn—2 sts dec.

Row 6: Sl 1, p11, turn.

Row 7: Sl 1, k2, ssk, k2, k2tog, k9 to marker; cut A—2 sts dec.

Stuff head with fiberfill.

Hat

Change to B and continue in the rnd.

Rnd 1: Knit—22 sts.

Rnds 2–4: Purl; cut B.

Rnds 5–10: With C, knit.

Rnd 11: K2, [k2tog, k2] 5 times—17 sts.

Rnd 12: Knit.

Stuff hat with fiberfill.

Rnd 13: K1, [k2tog, k2] 4 times—13 sts.

Rnd 14: Knit.

K2tog around until 6 sts rem.

Cut C, leaving a 5-inch tail.

Using tapestry needle, thread tail through rem sts and pull tight.

Ear
Make 2

Notes: *Ears are worked flat from bottom and up. On Rows 2 and 3, twist yo's from previous row by working tbl.*

With A, cast on 2 sts, leaving a 6-inch tail to sew ears to head.

Row 1: P1, yo, p1—3 sts.

Row 2: K1, yo, k1, yo, k1—5 sts.

Row 3: P5.

Row 4: K2, k2tog, k1—4 sts.

Row 5: P1, p2tog, p1—3 sts.

Row 6: Sk2p.

Cut yarn and fasten off. Weave in end.

Use cast-on tails to sew bottom of ears to each side of head.

Finishing

Face
Note: *Refer to photo for embroidery.*

With F, embroider a small st on each side of face for eyes.

With B, embroider a long st for mouth.

Scarf
With B, cast on 45 sts.

Knit 2 rows.

Bind off.

Weave in ends.

Tie scarf around neck and secure by tacking.

Twisted-Cord Hanger
Cut 30-inch strand of D. Fold in half and secure folded end to a stationary object. Twist yarn until it begins to double back on itself. Fold in half again with both ends tog, and allow to twist on itself. Thread cord through top of hat. Tie ends tog in a knot; trim ends close to knot. Rotate cord so that knot is inside hat. ●

Santa Ornament

The Christmas tree would not be complete without Santa! This clever design starts like a toe-up sock, then progresses to a beard, a jolly face and a hat.

Design by Jackie Daugherty for Annie's Signature Designs

Skill Level

 INTERMEDIATE

Finished Measurement

Height: 5 inches

Materials

- Lion Brand Yarn Jiffy (chunky weight; 100% acrylic; 135 yds/ 85g per skein): 1 skein white #100 (A)
- Lion Brand Yarn Vanna's Choice (worsted weight; 100% acrylic; 170 yds/100g per skein): 1 skein each pink #101 (B) and cranberry #180 (C)
- 1 yd black yarn for eyes
- Size 8 (5mm) double-point needles (set of 4) or size needed to obtain gauge
- Stitch markers
- Fiberfill
- White sewing thread and sewing needle
- 8 inches monofilament thread

Gauge

16 sts and 24 rnds = 4 inches/10cm in St st.

Exact gauge is not critical for this project.

Special Abbreviations

Knot Stitch (NS): K1, then [slip st back to LH needle, k1] twice.

Make Bobble (MB): Knit into the front, back and front of next st, turn; p3, turn; k3, turn; p3, turn; CDD.

Centered Double Decrease (CDD): Slip next 2 sts as if to k2tog, k1, p2sso to dec 2 sts.

Make 1 Left (M1L): Insert LH needle from front to back under horizontal strand between last st worked and next st on LH needle; knit through back of resulting loop.

Make 1 Right (M1R): Insert LH needle from back to front under horizontal strand between last st worked and next st on LH needle; knit into front of resulting loop.

Pattern Notes

Ornament is worked in the round from the beard to the top of the hat.

Weave in ends at color changes as you go.

Yarn amounts given will yield approximately 12 ornaments.

Ornament

Beard

With A, cast on 6 sts; distribute sts to 3 dpns. Mark beg of rnd and join, being careful not to twist sts.

Rnd 1: [K1, NS, k1, pm] twice—6 sts.

Rnd 2: [K1, M1R, k1, M1L, k1] twice—10 sts.

Rnd 3: *K1, NS; rep from * around.

Rnd 4: [K1, M1R, knit to 1 st before marker, M1L, k1] twice—14 sts.

Rnds 5–11: Rep Rnds 3 and 4, ending with Rnd 3; cut A—26 sts.

Face

With B and removing 2nd marker on first rnd, knit 4 rnds.

Next rnd: K6, MB, knit to end of rnd.

Knit 2 rnds. Cut B.

Hat

With A, knit 1 rnd.

Purl 3 rnds. Cut A.

Add Features to Face

Note: Refer to photo for placement of features.

Using 12-inch strand of C, make ⅜-inch straight st for mouth 2 rows below bobble (nose).

With black, make 2 straight sts for eyes.

With C, knit 7 rnds and on last rnd, dec 2 sts evenly spaced—24 sts.

Lightly stuff ornament with fiberfill.

Next rnd: [K8, pm] 3 times.

Knit 2 rnds.

Dec rnd: [Knit to 2 sts before marker, k2tog] around—21 sts.

Knit 3 rnds.

Rep [last 4 rnds] 5 times—6 sts.

Cut yarn, leaving a 5-inch tail.

Using tapestry needle, thread tail through rem sts and pull tight.

Weave in ends.

Finishing

Pompom
With A, cast on 1 st; MB in cast-on st, cut yarn, leaving a 6-inch tail and fasten off.

Using tails, sew bobble to end of hat.

Weave in ends.

Mustache
Wrap 8-inch strand of A around 2 fingers to form 2 loops.

With sewing needle and white thread, sew loops in place just below bobble.

Using photo as guide, fold top part of hat over; using C, tack folded hat in place.

Hanger
Attach 8-inch strand of monofilament to top of ornament for hanger. ●

O Christmas Tree

Deck the halls and dress the tree with these crocodile stitch trees. Once you learn this innovative technique, you'll want to make several more.

Design by Lena Skvagerson for Annie's Signature Designs

Skill Level

◼◼◼◻ INTERMEDIATE

Finished Measurements

Width at bottom: 3½ inches

Height: 3¾ inches

Materials

- Premier Yarns Deborah Norville Serenity Sock Solids (fingering weight; 50% wool/25% nylon/ 25% rayon; 230 yds/50g per skein): 1 skein soft white #5001, red #5003 or woodsy green #5007

  1 SUPER FINE

- Size 2 (2.75mm) knitting needles or size needed to obtain gauge

Gauge

30 sts and 56 rows = 4 inches/10cm in garter st.

To save time, take time to check gauge.

Special Abbreviation

Make Scale (MS)

Note: Work all 5 rows of scale before continuing across pat row.

Row 1 (RS): (K1, [yo, k1] 3 times) in next st, turn—7 sts.

Row 2: K7, turn.

Row 3: K3, (k1, [yo, k1] twice) in next st, k3, turn—11 sts.

Row 4: K1, bind off 9 sts very loosely, k1 (this is st that was knit before scale was started), pass last scale st over k1, turn—2 sts.

Row 5: K1, fold scale toward you so that WS of scale is visible (folding along base of cluster created on Row 1), pick up and knit 5 sts evenly spaced along folded edge of scale, ssk (last st of scale and next st on LH needle)—7 sts.

Do not turn; continue with pat row.

Pattern Notes

Tree is worked back and forth from the bottom up.

One skein will yield approximately 10 ornaments.

Tree

With color of choice, cast on 25 sts.

Knit 6 rows.

Row 1 (RS): K2tog, k1, MS, [sk2p, k1, MS] 3 times, k2tog—33 sts (4 scales).

Row 2: K2tog, k5, [sk2p, k5] 3 times, k2tog—25 sts.

Row 3: Knit.

Row 4: K1, [k2, k2tog] 6 times—19 sts.

Rows 5–8: Knit.

Rows 9 and 10: Work as for Rows 1 and 2, working sections in brackets twice—19 sts (3 scales).

Rows 11–16: Knit.

Rows 17–19: Rep Rows 1–3, working sections in brackets twice—19 sts (3 scales).

Row 20: K1, [k1, k2tog] 6 times—13 sts.

Rows 21–24: Knit.

Rows 25–27: Rep Rows 1–3, working sections in brackets once—13 sts (2 scales).

Row 28: K1, [k2tog] 6 times—7 sts.

Rows 29–32: Knit.

Row 33: K2tog, k1, MS, k2tog—9 sts (1 scale).

Row 34: K2tog, k5, k2tog—7 sts.

Row 35: K1, [k2tog] 3 times—4 sts

Row 36: K2tog twice; pass first st on RH needle over 2nd st—1 st.

Cut yarn. Fasten off last st.

Finishing
Weave in ends.

Twisted-Cord Hanger
Cut 30-inch strand of yarn. Fold in half and secure folded end to a stationary object. Twist yarn until it begins to double back on itself. Fold in half again with both ends tog and allow to twist on itself. Thread cord through top of tree. Tie ends tog in a knot; trim ends close to knot. Rotate cord so that knot ends up at back of tree. ●

Peppermint Wreath

All you need are small bits of red and white yarn to whip up this easy ornament wreath.

Design by Lena Skvagerson for Annie's Signature Designs

Skill Level

 INTERMEDIATE

Finished Measurement

Diameter: Approx 3¼ inches

Materials

- Premier Yarns Deborah Norville Serenity Sock Solids (fingering weight; 50% wool/25% nylon/25% rayon; 230 yds/50g per skein): 1 skein each soft white #5001 (A) and red #5003 (B)
- Size 1 (2.25mm) double-point needles (set of 4) or size needed to obtain gauge
- Fiberfill

1 SUPER FINE

Gauge

30 sts and 40 rnds = 4 inches/10cm in St st.

To save time, take time to check gauge.

Pattern Stitch

Stripe Pat

Rnds 1–8: With A, knit 4 rnds; with B, knit 4 rnds.

Rnds 9–20: [With A, knit 2 rnds; with B, knit 2 rnds] 3 times.

Rep Rnds 1–20 for pat.

Pattern Note

Amount of yarn listed will yield about 18 wreaths.

Wreath

With A, cast on 12 sts and distribute sts evenly on 3 dpns; mark beg of rnd and join, being careful not to twist.

*Work 20-rnd Stripe pat.

Stuff with fiberfill.

Rep from * 3 times.

Bind off.

Finishing

Weave in ends.

Sew cast-on edge to bound-off edge to form circle.

Twisted-Cord Hanger

Cut 40-inch strand of B. Fold in half and secure folded end to a stationary object. Twist yarn until it begins to double back on itself. Fold in half again with both ends tog and allow to twist on itself. Thread cord through wreath and tie ends tog in a knot. Trim ends close to knot.

Bow

With B, loosely cast on 60 sts.

Purl 1 row.

Bind off.

Weave in ends.

Tie in bow around bottom of hanger. ●

Nordic Snowflake

You'll enjoy diving into the world of stranded colorwork when you make this simple creation. Experiment with jewel-toned colors for a contemporary look.

Design by Lena Skvagerson for Annie's Signature Designs

Skill Level

 INTERMEDIATE

Finished Measurement

3¾ inches square

Materials

- Universal Yarn Uptown DK (DK weight; 100% acrylic; 273 yds/100g per skein): 1 skein each bittersweet #106 (A) and lily #102 (B)
- Size 7 (4.5mm) knitting needles or size needed to obtain gauge
- Fiberfill

Gauge

20 sts and 21 rows = 4 inches/10cm in 2-color stranded St st.

Exact gauge is not critical for this project.

Special Abbreviations

Purl in front and back (pfb): Purl in front and then in back of next st on LH needle.

Slip, slip, purl (ssp): Slip 2 sts 1 at a time kwise to RH needle; return sts to LH needle in turned position and p2tog tbl—a left leaning single dec.

Pattern Stitch

Snowflake

See chart, worked in 2-color stranded St st.

Special Technique
I-Cord: *Slip sts back to LH needle, k3, do not turn; rep from * until cord is desired length. Bind off.

Pattern Note
Amount of yarn listed will yield about 13 ornaments.

Square 1
Note: *Use A as MC and B as CC.*

With MC, cast on 3 sts.

Row 1 (WS): Pfb with MC; work Row 1 of chart, pfb with MC—5 sts.

Row 2 (RS): Kfb with MC, work Row 2 of chart, kfb with MC—7 sts.

Rows 3–14: Continuing to inc at edges as established, work through Row 14 of chart—31 sts.

Row 15: P2tog with MC, work Row 15 of chart, ssp with MC—29 sts.

Row 16: Ssk with MC, work Row 16 of chart, k2tog with MC—27 sts.

Rows 17–27: Continuing to dec at edges as established, work to end of chart—5 sts.

Row 28: With A, ssk, k1, k2tog—3 sts.

Cut B.

Hanger
With A, work 3-st I-Cord for approx 4 inches. Cut yarn and pull through rem sts.

Weave in ends.

Square 2
Note: *Use B as MC and A as CC.*

With B, cast on 3 sts.

Work as Square 1 but switch colors as indicated.

When 3 sts rem, bind off with B; do not work hanger.

Cut yarns.

Weave in ends.

Finishing
With WS of squares tog, sew 3 sides.

Stuff, then sew 4th side to close square.

Sew end of cord to top of square to form loop.

Weave in ends. ●

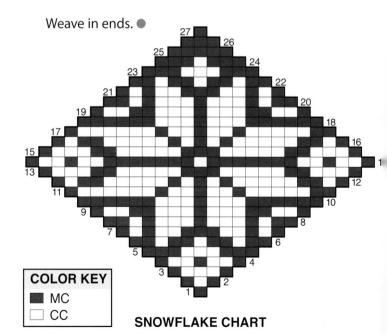

COLOR KEY
- ■ MC
- □ CC

SNOWFLAKE CHART

Redwork Ornaments

Enjoy the simple things in life and dress up a basic ornament with whimsical, embroidered accents.

Designs by Lena Skvagerson for Annie's Signature Designs

Skill Level

 INTERMEDIATE

Finished Measurement

Diameter: Approx 3¼ inches

Materials

- Universal Yarn Uptown DK (DK weight; 100% acrylic; 273 yds/100g per skein): 1 skein each bittersweet #106 (A) and lily #102 (B)
- Size 6 (4mm) double-point needles (set of 4) or size needed to obtain gauge
- Fiberfill

Gauge

18 sts and 20 rnds = 4 inches/10cm in St st.

To save time, take time to check gauge.

Special Technique

5-St I-Cord: *Do not turn, slide sts to other end of dpn, pull yarn across back, k5; rep from * until cord is desired length. Cut yarn. Thread tail through rem sts and pull tight.

Pattern Note

Amount of yarn listed will yield about 12 ornaments.

Ball With Bow

With B and leaving a 6-inch tail, cast on 10 sts; distribute sts on 3 dpns. Mark beg of rnd and join, being careful not to twist.

Rnd 1: Knit.

Rnd 2: *K1, yo; rep from * around—20 sts.

Rnd 3: Knit, working all yo's tbl.

Rnd 4: *K2, yo; rep from * around—30 sts.

Rnd 5: Knit, working all yo's tbl.

Rnd 6: *K3, yo; rep from * around—40 sts.

Rnds 7–11: Knit, working all yo's tbl.

Rnd 12: Change to A; knit.

Rnds 13 and 14: Purl. Cut A.

Rnd 15: With B, knit.

Rnds 16–19: Knit.

Rnd 20: *K2, k2tog; rep from * around—30 sts.

Rnd 21: Knit.

Rnd 22: *K1, k2tog; rep from * around—20 sts.

Rnd 23: Knit.

Rnd 24: K2tog around—10 sts.

Stuff with fiberfill.

Rnd 25: K2tog around—5 sts.

Hanger

Transfer all 5 sts to 1 dpn.

Work 5-St I-Cord approx 5 inches long.

Sew end of I-Cord to top of ball to form loop.

Bow

With A, loosely cast on 60 sts.

Bind off.

Weave in ends.

Sew center ¼ inch of knit strand to red stripe in center of ball.

Tie a bow.

Finishing

Weave cast-on tail through cast-on sts and pull tight to close hole.

Weave in ends.

Ball With Stars

Rnds 1–11: Work as for Ball With Bow.

Rnds 12–14: Continuing with B, knit.

Rnds 15–25: Work as for Ball With Bow. Cut B.

Hanger

Change to A; complete hanger as for Ball With Bow.

Finishing

Weave cast-on tail through cast-on sts and pull tight to close hole.

Weave in ends.

Stars

With A, embroider stars randomly around ball as shown in photo. ●

Angel Choir

Change up the color of each body to create your very own assembly of angels. They will brighten the tree and warm your heart!

Design by Jodi Lewanda

Skill Level

■■■□ INTERMEDIATE

Finished Measurement

5½ inches tall

Materials

- DK weight yarn: Approx 20 yds white (MC) and 25 yds in color of choice (CC)
- Size 2 (2.75mm) double-point needles (set of 5) or size needed to obtain gauge
- Stitch marker
- Fiberfill
- 1 yd ⅜-inch-wide wired ribbon
- 12 inches ⅛-inch-wide wired ribbon

Gauge

28 sts and 32 rnds = 4 inches/10cm in St st.

To save time, take time to check gauge.

Special Technique

3-Needle Bind-Off: With RS tog and needles parallel, use a 3rd needle to knit a st from the front needle tog with 1 from the back. *Knit tog a st from the front and back needles, then pass the first st on RH needle over the 2nd to bind off. Rep from * across, then fasten off last st.

Pattern Note

Angel is worked at a denser gauge on smaller needles than is usual for DK-weight yarn.

Angel

Head

With MC, cast on 4 sts.

Set-up row (RS): Kfb in each st across—8 sts.

Divide sts onto 4 dpns; pm for beg of rnd and join, being careful not to twist sts.

Rnd 1: Knit.

Rnd 2: [Kfb, k1] 4 times—12 sts.

Rnds 3 and 5: Knit.

Rnd 4: [Kfb, k2] 4 times—16 sts.

Rnd 6: [Kfb, k3] 4 times—20 sts.

Rnds 7–12: Knit.

Rnd 13: [K2tog, k3] 4 times—16 sts.

Stuff head with fiberfill to desired fullness.

Rnd 14: [K2tog, k2] 4 times—12 sts.

Rnd 15: [K2tog, k1] 4 times—8 sts.

Cut MC.

Body
Join CC.

Rnd 16: Knit.

Rnd 17: [K1, kfb] 4 times—12 sts.

Rnd 18: [K2, kfb] 4 times—16 sts.

Rnds 19 and 21: Knit.

Rnd 20: [K3, kfb] 4 times—20 sts.

Rnd 22: [K4, kfb] 4 times—24 sts.

Rnds 23 and 24: Knit.

Rnd 25: [K5, kfb] 4 times—28 sts.

Rnds 26 and 27: Knit.

Rnd 28: [K6, kfb] 4 times—32 sts.

Rnds 29 and 30: Knit.

Rnd 31: [K7, kfb] 4 times—36 sts.

Rnds 32 and 33: Knit.

Rnd 34: [K8, kfb] 4 times—40 sts.

Rnds 35 and 36: Knit.

Rnd 37: [K9, kfb] 4 times—44 sts.

Rnds 38 and 39: Knit.

Rnd 40: [K10, kfb] 4 times—48 sts.

Rnds 41–43: Knit.

Rnd 44: [K11, kfb] 4 times—52 sts.

Rnds 45 and 46: Knit.

Rnd 47 (eyelet rnd): *K2tog, yo; rep from * around.

Rnds 48 and 49: Knit.

Rnd 50: Purl.

Rnd 51: Knit.

Bind off all sts pwise.

Wings
Note: Wings are worked back and forth in rows.

*Using MC, cast on 22 sts.

Rows 1 and 2: Knit.

Row 3: Bind off 3 sts, knit to last 2 sts, kfb, k1—20 sts.

Row 4: Knit.

Rows 5–8: Rep [Rows 3 and 4] twice—16 sts.

Row 9: Bind off 2 sts, knit to last 2 sts, k2tog—13 sts.

Row 10: Knit.

Rows 11–16: Rep [Rows 9 and 10] 3 times—4 sts.

Cut yarn, leaving sts on spare needle.

Rep from * for 2nd wing.

Join the 2 sets of sts using 3-Needle Bind-Off.

Tack wings to back of angel, positioning top of seam at neck.

Finishing
Weave in ends.

Starting at front of angel's skirt, lace ⅜-inch-wide ribbon through eyelets. Tie ribbon into a bow and trim.

Insert ⅛-inch-wide ribbon through top of head and tie for hanger. ●

Wish Upon a Star

The tree would not be complete without an assortment of these delightfully delicate fingering-weight stars.

Designs by Lena Skvagerson for Annie's Signature Designs

Skill Level

■■■□ INTERMEDIATE

Finished Measurements

Small star: Approx 4½ inches from point to point
Large star: Approx 6 inches from point to point

Materials

- Premier Yarns Deborah Norville Serenity Sock Solids (fingering weight; 50% wool/25% nylon/ 25% rayon; 230 yds/50g per skein): 1 skein soft white #5001

  1 SUPER FINE

- Size 1 (2.25mm) knitting needles

Gauge

30 sts and 56 rows = 4 inches/10cm in garter st.

Exact gauge is not critical for this project.

Pattern Notes

Stars are formed by working short-row wedges. When working short rows, do not wrap the turning stitch—the holes are deliberate.

One skein will yield approximately 20 small stars or 9 large stars.

Small Star

Cast on 10 sts.

Knit 1 row.

Row 1 and all WS rows: Knit.

Row 2 (RS): K1, yo, k2tog, knit to last st, turn.

Rows 4, 6, 8, 10, 12 and 14: K1, yo, k2tog, knit to 1 st before previous turn, turn.

Row 16: Bind off 2 sts, [yo, pass st on RH needle over, k1, pass st on RH needle over] twice, yo, pass st on RH needle over, [k1, yo] 5 times—10 sts.

Rep [Rows 1–16] 5 times.

Bind off.

Sew cast-on and bound-off edges tog.

Weave in ends.

Twisted-Cord Hanger

Cut 12-inch strand of yarn. Twist yarn until it resists, then fold in half, allowing ends to twist tog, forming a cord. Thread cord through a star point, then tie in knot. Trim ends.

Large Star

Cast on 15 sts.

Knit 1 row.

Row 1 and all WS rows: Knit.

Row 2 (RS): Knit to last st, turn.

Row 4 and all RS rows through Row 26: Knit to 1 st before previous turn, turn.

Row 28: Bind off 1 st, [yo, pass st on RH needle over, k1, pass st on RH needle over] 6 times (7 sts rem on LH needle), *yo, k1; rep from * to end—15 sts.

Rep [Rows 1–28] 5 times.

Bind off.

Sew cast-on and bound-off edges tog.

Weave in ends.

Twisted-Cord Hanger

Cut 14-inch strand of yarn. Twist yarn until it resists, then fold in half, allowing ends to twist tog, forming a cord. Thread cord through a star point, then tie in knot. Trim ends. ●

Opulent Openwork Ornaments

Dress the tree with these elegant lace-covered ball ornaments! They can be made with lace- or fingering-weight yarns, with or without beads. Experiment with shimmery yarns or smooth variegated varieties to create a different look every time.

Designs by Kara Gott Warner for Annie's Signature Designs

Skill Level

 INTERMEDIATE

Finished Measurements

Circumference: Approx 8½ (10) inches

Materials

- Lace weight yarn: Approx 25–30 yds or fingering weight yarn: Approx 40 yds
- Size 1 (2.25mm) double-point needles (set of 4) or size needed to obtain gauge
- Ball ornament: 2¾ (3¼) inches in diameter
- 36 seed beads (for beaded version only)
- Bead threader (for beaded version only)
- ¼-inch-wide ribbon for hanger (optional)
- Size B/1 (2.25mm) crochet hook for hanger (optional)
- Stitch marker
- Size 1 (2.25mm) knitting needles

0 LACE

1 SUPER FINE

Gauge

32 sts and 42 rnds = 4 inches/10cm in St st with lace-weight yarn.

28 sts and 37 rnds = 4 inches/10cm in St st with fingering-weight yarn.

To save time, take time to check gauge.

Special Abbreviation

Slide bead (SB): Slide bead up from yarn ball, ready for next st.

Pattern Notes

Cover is worked in the round from the top down.

When 30 stitches remain on the needles, cover is slipped over the top of the ornament. The cast-on edge encircles the neck of the ornament with a snug fit; carefully stretch as necessary to fit.

Pattern includes a basic version and a beaded version.

Cover can be worked with either lace-weight yarn or fingering-weight yarn. A cover worked with fingering-weight yarn will fit a larger ornament. Experiment with various-size Christmas balls for desired fit.

Basic Ornament Cover

Leaving a 6-inch tail, cast on 12 sts; distribute sts on 3 dpns. Mark beg of rnd and join, being careful not to twist.

Increasing Half

Rnd 1: K1-tbl around.

Rnd 2: [Yo, k2] 6 times around—18 sts.

Rnd 3: [Yo, k1, k2tog] 6 times.

Rnd 4: [Yo, k3] 6 times—24 sts.

Rnd 5: [Yo, k2, k2tog] 6 times.

Rnd 6: [Yo, k4] 6 times—30 sts.

Rnd 7: [Yo, k3, k2tog] 6 times.

Rnd 8: [Yo, k5] 6 times—36 sts.

Rnd 9: [Yo, k4, k2tog] 6 times.

Rnd 10: [Yo, k6] 6 times—42 sts.

Rnd 11: [Yo, k5, k2tog] 6 times.

Rnd 12: [Yo, k7] 6 times—48 sts.

Rnd 13: [Yo, k6, k2tog] 6 times.

Rnd 14: [Yo, k8] 6 times—54 sts.

Rnd 15: [Yo, k7, k2tog] 6 times.

Rnd 16: [Yo, k9] 6 times—60 sts.

Rnd 17: [Yo, k8, k2tog] 6 times.

Rnd 18: [Yo, k10] 6 times—66 sts.

Rnd 19: [Yo, k9, k2tog] 6 times.

Rnd 20: [Yo, k11] 6 times—72 sts.

Rnd 21: [Yo, k10, k2tog] 6 times.

Rnd 22: [Yo, k12] 6 times—78 sts.

Decreasing Half

Rnd 1: [K11, k2tog] 6 times—72 sts.

Rnd 2: [Yo, k10, k2tog] 6 times.

Rnd 3: [K10, k2tog] 6 times—66 sts.

Rnd 4: [Yo, k9, k2tog] 6 times.

Rnd 5: [K9, k2tog] 6 times—60 sts.

Rnd 6: [Yo, k8, k2tog] 6 times.

Rnd 7: [K8, k2tog] 6 times—54 sts.

Rnd 8: [Yo, k7, k2tog] 6 times.

Rnd 9: [K7, k2tog] 6 times—48 sts.

Rnd 10: [Yo, k6, k2tog] 6 times.

Rnd 11: [K6, k2tog] 6 times—42 sts.

Rnd 12: [Yo, k5, k2tog] 6 times.

Rnd 13: [K5, k2tog] 6 times—36 sts.

Rnd 14: [Yo, k4, k2tog] 6 times.

Rnd 15: [K4, k2tog] 6 times—30 sts.

Continue with Finishing.

Beaded Ornament Cover

With threader, thread 36 beads onto ball of yarn. Beads wait on yarn until needed—continue to slide them down yarn as needed.

Increasing Half

Leaving a 6-inch tail, cast on 12 sts; distribute sts to 3 dpns. Mark beg of rnd and join, being careful not to twist.

Rnds 1–5: Work as for basic version—24 sts.

Rnd 6 (bead rnd): [Yo, k1, SB, p1, k2] 6 times—30 sts.

Rnds 7–22: Work as for basic version, adding beads every 6 rnds as follows:

Rnd 12 (bead rnd): [Yo, k1, SB, p1, k5] 6 times—48 sts.

Rnd 18 (bead rnd): [Yo, k1, SB, p1, k8] 6 times—66 sts.

Decreasing Half

Rnds 1–15: Work as for basic version, but add beads on Rnd 2, then every 6 rnds as follows:

Rnd 2 (bead rnd): [Yo, k1, SB, p1, k8, k2tog] 6 times.

Rnd 8 (bead rnd): [Yo, k1, SB, p1, k5, k2tog] 6 times.

Rnd 14 (bead rnd): [Yo, k1, SB, p1, k2, k2tog] 6 times.

Finishing (Both Versions)

Slide the cover snugly over the top of ornament with the 30 rem sts still on dpns.

Cut yarn, leaving an 8-inch tail. Using tapestry needle, thread tail through rem sts and pull tight.

Carefully weave in both ends as invisibly as possible.

Hanger

Option #1: Cut a 10-inch piece of ¼-inch-wide ribbon; thread through top of ornament, then tie in a bow. Trim excess ribbon.

Option #2: Use crochet hook to create a 6-inch crochet chain; thread through top of ornament, then tie in bow. ●

Drop Stitch Delight

This beaded drop-stitch ornament is a great way to show off your colorful Christmas balls. A little yarn really goes a long way—all you need is a small amount of festive fingering-weight yarn from your stash and you'll be good to go!

Design by Kara Gott Warner for Annie's Signature Designs

Skill Level

 INTERMEDIATE

Finished Measurement

Circumference: Approx 8½–9 inches

Materials

- Fingering weight yarn: Approx 30 yds
- Size 1 (2.25mm) double-point needles (set of 4) or size needed to obtain gauge
- Ball ornament: Approx 2¾ inches in diameter
- 36 seed beads
- Bead threader
- ¼-inch-wide ribbon for hanger (optional)
- Size B/1 (2.25mm) crochet hook for hanger (optional)
- Stitch marker

Gauge

32 sts and 42 rnds = 4 inches/10cm in St st.

To save time, take time to check gauge.

Special Abbreviation

Make 1 Left (M1L): Insert LH needle from front to back under horizontal strand between last st worked and next st on LH needle; knit through back of resulting loop.

Pattern Notes

Cover is worked in the round from the bottom up.

When cover measures 3 inches, the cast-on edge is slipped over the top of the ornament. The cast-on edge may be a bit snug, so stretch it carefully as needed.

Experiment with various-size Christmas ball ornaments for desired fit.

Ornament Cover

With threader, thread 36 beads onto ball of yarn. Beads wait on yarn until needed—continue to slide them down yarn as needed.

Leaving a 6-inch tail, cast on 36 sts; distribute sts to 3 dpns. Mark beg of rnd and join, being careful not to twist.

Rnds 1–5: [K2, p2] 9 times.

Rnd 6: [K2, p1, M1, p1] 9 times—45 sts.

Rnds 7 and 8: [K2, p1, k1, p1] 9 times.

Rnd 9 (bead rnd): [K2, p1, slide bead up close to RH needle and knit bead with next st, p1] 9 times.

Rnds 10–12: [K2, p1, k1, p1] 9 times.

Rnds 13–24: Rep [Rnds 9–12] 3 times.

Rnd 25: [K2, p1, drop next st and let it run down to Rnd 2, p1] 9 times—36 sts.

Work in 2x2 rib until piece measures 3 inches.

Do not bind off.

Finishing

Slide the cover snugly over the top of the ornament with sts still on dpns.

Cut yarn, leaving an 8-inch tail.

Using tapestry needle, thread tail through rem sts and pull tight around neck of ornament.

Using tapestry needle, thread cast-on tail through cast-on edge and pull tight around bottom of ornament.

Carefully weave in both ends as invisibly as possible.

Hanger

Option #1: Cut a 12-inch piece of ¼-inch-wide ribbon; thread through top of ornament, then tie in a bow. Trim excess ribbon.

Option #2: Use crochet hook to create a 6-inch crochet chain; thread through top of ornament, then tie in a bow. ●

I Gave You My Heart

With just two colors, you can test drive your colorworking skills on this sweet little sweater.

Design by Angelique den Brok

Skill Level

 INTERMEDIATE

Finished Measurements

Approx 3 inches long x 4½ inches wide (excluding hanger)

Materials

- DROPS Baby Merino (sport weight; 100% merino wool; 191 yds/50g per ball): Small amount each off-white #02 (A) and red #16 (B)

2 FINE

- Size 2 (2.75mm) double-point needles (set of 5) or size needed to obtain gauge
- 3 stitch holders or waste yarn
- Stitch marker
- 7-inch-long off-white pipe cleaner

Gauge

28 sts and 36 rnds = 4 inches/10cm in St st.

Gauge is not critical for this project.

Special Abbreviation

Make 1 (M1): Insert LH needle from front to back under horizontal strand between last st worked and next st on LH needle, knit through back of resulting loop.

Pattern Stitches

1x1 Rib (even number of sts)

All rnds: *K1, p1; rep from * around.

Heart Pat

Note: A chart is provided for those preferring to work color pat from a chart.

Rnd 1: *K4 A, k1 B, k3 A; rep from * around.

Rnd 2: *K3 A, k3 B, k2 A; rep from * around.

Rnd 3: *K2 A, k5 B; rep from * around.

Rnd 4: *K1 A, k7 B, k3 A; rep from * around.

Rnd 5: *K2 A, k2 B, k1 A, k2 B, k1 A; rep from * around.

Pattern Notes

Patterned yoke is worked with 2-color stranded stockinette stitch. Carry color not in use loosely on wrong side of fabric. When working more than 4 stitches in a row with same color, catch carried yarn with working yarn to avoid long float.

Yarn listed will yield approximately 8 ornaments.

Body

With A, cast on 38 sts; distribute sts to 4 dpns. Mark beg of rnd and join, being careful not to twist.

Work 4 rnds in 1x1 Rib.

Knit 12 rnds.

Division rnd: [Bind off 4 sts, k15 (including st on RH needle from bind-off)] twice.

Cut yarn, leaving a 6-inch tail.

Transfer each set of sts to separate holder or strand of waste yarn for front and back.

Sleeves

With dpns and A, cast on 16 sts; mark beg of rnd and join, being careful not to twist.

Work 4 rnds in 1x1 Rib.

Knit 9 rnds.

Next rnd: Knit to last 2 sts, bind off 4 sts.

Cut yarn, leaving a 6-inch tail.

Transfer sts to holder or strand of waste yarn.

Rep for 2nd sleeve but do not cut yarn and leave sts on dpns.

Yoke

Joining rnds: Continuing with yarn from 2nd sleeve, knit across sleeve sts; k15 front sts from holder; k12 sleeve sts from holder; work across back sts on holder as follows: k1, M1, k5, pm for new beg of rnd, k8, M1, k1; knit around to beg-of-rnd marker—56 sts.

Rearrange sts on dpns as desired.

Work 5-rnd Heart Pat. Cut B.

With A, knit 2 rnds.

Dec rnd: *K2, k2tog; rep from * around—42 sts.

Next rnd: Knit.

Dec rnd: *K1, k2tog; rep from * around—28 sts.

Work 4 rnds in 1x1 Rib.

Bind off in pat.

Finishing

Sew underarms closed.

Weave in ends.

Block sweater to even out color pat.

Using yarn tails at armholes, close underarm openings.

Weave in ends.

Block sweater.

Make Hanger

Bend pipe cleaner into a coat hanger as follows: Lay pipe cleaner horizontally on table. Bend rightmost inch of pipe cleaner down, then flush with rest of pipe cleaner. Bend again 2 inches from first bend (again making flush), so that there is a longer section on top, sticking out about ¾ inch from bent section. Bend top section in half, then wrap once around middle to secure lower folded part of hanger. Bend the rem top section into a small hook.

Insert hanger into sweater and adjust the position of the lower part of hanger for a good fit. ●

COLOR KEY

☐ A

■ B

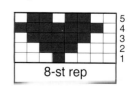

8-st rep

HEART PAT CHART

Walking in a Winter Wonderland

Even though this sweater is tiny, once you've knitted it you'll have mastered all the techniques needed to knit your own full-size traditional Icelandic sweater.

Design by Angelique den Brok

Skill Level

 INTERMEDIATE

Finished Measurements

Approx 3 inches long x 4½ inches wide (excluding hanger)

Materials

- DROPS Baby Merino (sport weight; 100% merino wool; 191 yds/50g per ball): Small amount each electric blue #33 (A), turquoise #32 (B), cerise #08 (C) and off-white #02 (D)
- Size 2 (2.75mm) double-point needles (set of 5) or size needed to obtain gauge
- 3 stitch holders or waste yarn
- Stitch marker
- 7-inch-long off-white pipe cleaner

2 FINE

Gauge

28 sts and 36 rnds = 4 inches/10cm in St st.

Gauge is not critical for this project.

Special Abbreviation

Make 1 (M1): Insert LH needle from front to back under horizontal strand between last st worked and next st on LH needle, knit into back of resulting loop.

Pattern Stitches

1x1 Rib (even number of sts)

All rnds: *K1, p1; rep from * around.

Yoke Pat

Note: A chart is provided for those preferring to work color pat from a chart.

Rnd 1: *K3 A, k1 B; rep from * around.

Rnd 2: *K1 B, k1 A, k2 B; rep from * around.

Rnd 3: *K3 B, k1 C; rep from * around.

Rnd 4: *K1 C, k1 B, k2 C; rep from * around.

Rnd 5: *K3 C, k1 D; rep from * around.

Rnd 6: *K1 D, k1 C, k2 D; rep from * around.

Pattern Notes

Multicolored yoke is worked with 2-color stranded stockinette stitch. Carry color not in use loosely on wrong side of fabric.

Yarn listed will yield approximately 8 ornaments.

Body

With A, cast on 38 sts; distribute sts to 4 dpns. Mark beg of rnd and join, being careful not to twist.

Work 4 rnds in 1x1 Rib.

Knit 12 rnds.

Division rnd: [Bind off 4 sts, k15 (including st on RH needle from bind-off)] twice.

Cut yarn, leaving a 6-inch tail.

Transfer each set of sts to separate holder or strand of waste yarn for front and back.

Sleeves

With dpns and A, cast on 16 sts; mark beg of rnd and join, being careful not to twist.

Work 4 rnds in 1x1 Rib.

Knit 9 rnds.

Next rnd: Knit to last 2 sts, bind off 4 sts—12 sts.

Cut yarn, leaving a 6-inch tail.

Transfer sts to holder or strand of waste yarn.

Rep for 2nd sleeve, but do not cut yarn and leave sts on dpns.

Yoke

Joining rnds: Continuing with yarn from 2nd sleeve and using same dpns, knit across sleeve sts, k15 front sts from holder; k12 sleeve sts from holder; work across back sts on holder as follows: k1, M1, k6, pm for new beg of rnd, k7, M1, k1; knit around to beg of rnd marker—56 sts. Rearrange sts on dpns as desired.

Joining new colors when needed, work 6-rnd Yoke Pat.

With D, knit 2 rnds.

Dec rnd: *K2, k2tog; rep from * around—42 sts.

Next rnd: Knit.

Dec rnd: *K1, k2tog; rep from * around—28 sts.

Work 4 rnds in 1x1 Rib.

Bind off in pat.

Finishing

Using tails at armholes, sew underarms closed.

Weave in ends.

Block sweater to even out color pat.

Make Hanger

Bend pipe cleaner into a coat hanger as follows: Lay pipe cleaner horizontally on table. Bend rightmost inch of pipe cleaner down, then flush with rest of pipe cleaner. Bend again 2 inches from first bend (again making flush), so that there is a longer section on top, sticking out about ¾ inch from bent section. Bend top section in half, then wrap once around middle to secure lower folded part of hanger. Bend the rem top section into a small hook.

Insert hanger into sweater and adjust the position of the lower part of hanger for a good fit. ●

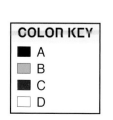

COLOR KEY
■ A
▨ B
◆ C
□ D

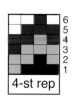

6
5
4
3
2
1

4-st rep

YOKE PAT CHART

Cabled Christmas Stocking

Trim the tree with these sweet little stockings in your choice of two whimsical stitch patterns.

Design by E. J. Slayton

Skill Level

 EASY

Finished Measurement

Approx 6 inches long

Materials

- Fingering weight yarn: Approx 50 yds per stocking in color of choice
- Size 1 (2.25mm) double-point needles (set of 4) and/or 2 (24-inch) circular needles or size needed to obtain gauge
- Stitch markers
- Cable needle
- Size B/1 (2.25mm) crochet hook

1 SUPER FINE

Gauge

28 sts and 40 rnds = 4 inches/10cm in St st.

Exact gauge is not critical for this project.

Special Abbreviations

Make 1 (M1): Inc by making a backward loop over RH needle.

2 over 2 Right Cross (2/2 RC): Sl 2 sts to cn and hold in back; k2, k2 from cn.

2 over 2 Left Cross (2/2 LC): Sl 2 sts to cn and hold in front; k2, k2 from cn.

Special Technique

3-Needle Bind-Off: With WS facing out and needles parallel, using a 3rd needle, knit tog a st from the front needle with 1 from the back. *Knit tog a st from the front and back needles, and slip the first st over the 2nd to bind off. Rep from * across, then fasten off last st.

Pattern Stitches

Note: Charts are provided for pat placement and for those preferring to work pat sts from charts.

Cable (12-st panel)

Rnds 1–3: P2, k8, p2.

Rnd 4: P2, 2/2 RC, 2/2 LC, p2.

Rnds 5–8: Rep Rnds 1–4.

Rnds 9–11: P2, k8, p2.

Rnd 12: P2, 2/2 LC, 2/2 RC, p2.

Rnds 13–16: Rep Rnds 9–12.

Rep Rnds 1–16 for pat.

Hearts (27-st panel)

Rnd 1: P1, k11, p3, k11, p1.

Rnd 2: P2, k9, p5, k9, p2.

Rnd 3: P1, k11, p3, k11, p1.

Rnd 4: K3, [p2, k3] twice, p1, k3, [p2, k3] twice.

Rnd 5: K2, p4, k1, p4, k5, p4, k1, p4, k2.

Rnd 6: K1, p2, k2, p3, k2, p2, k3, p2, k2, p3, k2, p2, k1.

Rnd 7: K1, p2, k3, p1, [k3, p2] twice, k3, p1, k3, p2, k1.

Rnd 8: K2, p2, [k5, p2] 3 times, k2.

Rnd 9: [K3, p2] twice, k7, [p2, k3] twice.

Rnd 10: K4, p2, k1, p2, k9, p2, k1, p2, k4.

Rnd 11: K5, p3, k11, p3, k5.

Rnd 12: K6, [p1, k6] 3 times.

Rep Rnds 1–12 for pat.

Pine Trees (27-st panel)

Note: Pine Trees panel may be worked in place of Hearts panel; work Rnds 1–50.

Rnds 1 and 2: K27.

Rnds 3 and 4: K6, p1, k13, p1, k6.

Rnds 5 and 6: K5, p1, k1, p1, k11, p1, k1, p1, k5.

Rnd 7: K27.

Rnd 8: K4, p1 k3, p1, k9, p1, k3, p1, k4.

Rnd 9: K4, p2, k1, p2, k9, p2, k1, p2, k4.

Rnd 10: K5, p1, k1, p1, k11, p1, k1, p1, k5.

Rnd 11: K3, p1, k5, p1, k7, p1, k5, p1, k3.

Rnd 12: [K3, p2] twice, k7, [p2, k3] twice.

Rnd 13: K4, p2, k1, p2, k9, p2, k1, p2, k4.

Rnd 14: [K2, p1] twice, k1, p1, k2, p1, k5, p1, k2, p1, k1, [p1, k2] twice.

Rnd 15: K2, p2, [k5, p2] 3 times, k2.

Rnd 16: [K3, p2] twice, k7, [p2, k3] twice.

Rnd 17: K1, p1, k2, p2, k1, p2, k2, p1, k3, p1, k2, p2, k1, p2, k2, p1, k1.

Rnd 18: K1, p2, k2, p1, k1, p1, k2, p2, k3, p2, k2, p1, k1, p1, k2, p2, k1.

Rnd 19: K2, p2, [k5, p2] 3 times, k2.

Rnd 20: [K3, p2] twice, k7, [p2, k3] twice.

Rnd 21: K4, p2, k1, p2, k9, p2, k1, p2, k4.

Rnd 22: K5, p1, k1, p1, k11, p1, k1, p1, k5.

Rnds 23 and 24: K6, p1, k13, p1, k6.

Rnds 25 and 26: K27.

Rnds 27–50: Rep Rnds 3–26.

Pattern Notes

Stocking is worked in the round from the cuff to the toe.

Stocking may be worked on a set of double-point needles or with the stitches divided on two 24-inch circular needles.

The heel is an "afterthought" heel that is initially worked with waste yarn that will be removed later, at which point the heel is completed.

Knitter has option of working 1 of 2 center front panels—the Hearts panel or the Pine Trees panel.

Stocking

Cast on 46 sts; distribute sts to 3 dpns or 2 circular needles, divided as follows: 19 sts on first needle (Needle 1) and rem 27 sts either on 2 dpns or on 2nd circular needle; mark beg of rnd and join without twisting.

Cuff

Work 6 rnds in 1x1 rib.

Leg

Rnd 1 (inc): P2, [k1, M1] 4 times, p2, k3, p2, [k1, M1] 4 times, p2; work Rnd 1 of Hearts (Pine Trees) panel—54 sts with 27 sts on Needle 1 and 27 sts on rem needle(s).

Rnd 2: Working Rnd 2 of each pat, work 12-st Cable panel, k3, work 12-st Cable panel; work 27-st Heart (Pine Trees) panel.

Rnds 3–33: Work pats as established, ending with Rnd 1 of Cable pat.

Rnd 34: With waste yarn, knit across first 27 sts on Needle 1; drop waste yarn and slide sts back to other end of needle; with working yarn, work all sts in pat around.

Rnds 35–48: Work pats as set, ending with Rnd 16 of Cable.

Rnd 49: P2, k8, p2, k3, p2, k8, p2; k27.

Rnd 50 (dec): P2, ssk twice, k2tog twice, p2, k3, p2, ssk twice, k2tog twice, p2 (19 sts on Needle 1); k27—46 sts.

Toe

Rnd 1: Sl 2 sts onto beg and end of first needle so there are 23 sts on Needle 1 and 23 sts on rem needle(s); [k1, ssk, k17, k2tog, k1] twice—42 sts.

Rnd 2: Knit.

Rnd 3: K1, ssk, knit to last 3 sts of Needle 1, k2tog, k1; k1, ssk, knit to last 3 sts of rnd, k2tog, k1.

Rnd 4: Knit.

Rnds 5–12: Rep [Rnds 3 and 4] 4 times—22 sts.

Rnd 13: Rep Rnd 3—18 sts.

Transfer sts to 2 dpns so that there are 9 needles on Needle 1 and 9 sts on Needle 2.

Carefully turn stocking inside out, leaving sts on needles. Close toe using 3-Needle Bind-Off.

Heel

Remove waste yarn, sliding sts onto needles. Pick up an extra st if needed, so there are 27 sts on Needle 1 and 27 sts on rem needle(s)—54 sts.

Rnd 1: Knit and dec 4 sts across each cable as for Rnd 50—38 sts.

Rnd 2: K1, ssk, knit to last 3 sts of Needle 1, k2tog, k1; k1, ssk, knit to last 3 sts of rnd, k2tog, k1.

Rnd 3: Knit.

Rnds 4–9: Rep [Rnds 2 and 3] 3 times—22 sts.

Rnd 10: Rep Rnd 2—18 sts.

Transfer sts to 2 dpns so that there are 9 needles on Needle 1 and 9 sts on Needle 2.

Carefully turn stocking inside out, leaving sts on needles. Close heel using 3-Needle Bind-Off.

Hanger

Using crochet hook, attach yarn at center back of cuff; work a chain that measures approx 1½ inches. Fasten off and sew end of chain to inside of stocking. ●

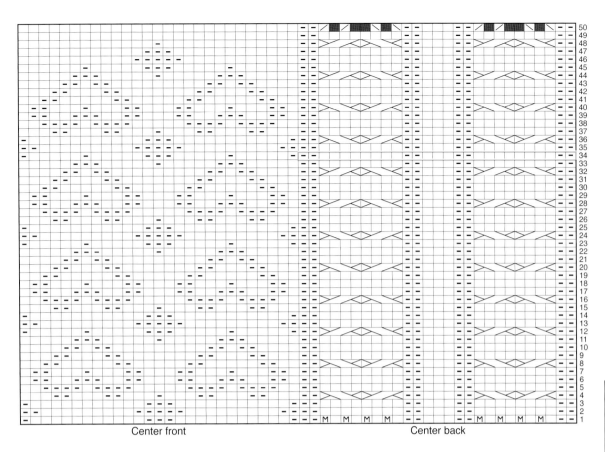

Center front   Center back

CABLE & HEARTS CHART

Note: On Rnd 34, work sts outlined in blue with waste yarn (for heel), then with working yarn.

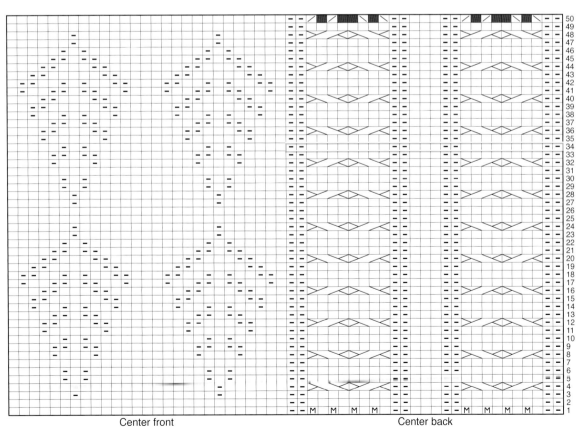

Center front   Center back

CABLE & PINE TREES CHART

Note: On Rnd 34, work sts outlined in blue with waste yarn (for heel), then with working yarn.

Merry & Bright Stockings

This cute miniature Christmas stocking can be used as an ornament or tied on a package!

Design by Marji LaFreniere

Skill Level

 INTERMEDIATE

Finished Measurements

Approx 1½ inches wide across leg x 3½ inches long

Materials

- Fingering weight yarn: Small amounts smooth yarn in a variety of colors
- Fingering weight yarn: 2–3 yds white angora or fine mohair for top edge
- Size 2 (2.75mm) double-point needles (set of 5)

1 SUPER FINE

Gauge

32 sts and 42 rnds = 4 inches/10cm in St st.

Exact gauge is not critical for this project.

Pattern Stitch

Corrugated Rib (multiple of 4 sts)

Pat rnd: K2 B, p2 A.

Pattern Note

Stocking is worked in the round from the cuff down. Top edge is worked with a fuzzy angora or mohair yarn, after which the rest of the stocking is worked with assorted colors of fingering weight yarn. Patterns used in samples are charted, but use any color patterns you desire that are multiples of 2, 3 or 4 stitches.

Stocking

Cuff

Using fuzzy white yarn (angora or mohair), cast on 24 sts and distribute to 3 dpns. Mark beg of rnd and join without twisting.

Purl 3 rnds. Cut fuzzy yarn.

Change to fingering weight yarn in color A; knit 1 rnd.

Using 2 colors of choice (A and B), work 3 rnds in Corrugated Rib.

With A, knit 1 rnd.

Leg

Next 16 rnds: Changing colors as desired, knit every round. Optional: Work Sock Chart A or Sock Chart B or stitch pat of choice.

Cut yarn.

Heel

Slip last 6 sts of rnd and first 7 sts of rnd onto a needle for heel. Leave rem 11 sts on 2 dpns while working heel.

Row 1 (RS): With color of choice, knit across 13 heel sts, turn.

Row 2 (WS): K6, p1, k6.

Row 3: P6, k1, p6.

Rep [Rows 2 and 3] 3 times.

Slip 6 heel sts onto another dpn and fold heel in half with RS sides tog (i.e., with St st facing out). Join sts from each needle using 3-Needle Bind-Off (see page 19), then bind off last st. Cut yarn and fasten off. Flip heel right side out.

Foot

Rejoin yarn to continue stocking as follows:

With RS facing, beg at center heel and using color of choice, pick up and knit 1 st at center heel, then pick up and knit 6 sts along side of heel; knit in established pat (if any) across 11 instep sts; pick up and knit 6 sts along other side of heel, redistributing sts onto 3 dpns as you go—24 sts.

Maintaining color pat as established, work 6 or 7 rnds even. Cut yarns.

Toe

Using color of choice, knit 1 rnd.

Dec rnd: [K1, k2tog] 8 times—16 sts.

Knit 2 rnds.

Last rnd: K2tog around—8 sts.

Cut yarn, leaving a 5-inch tail.

Using tapestry needle, thread tail through rem sts, and pull tight.

Finishing

Weave in ends.

Hanger

Using desired colors, make 2 pompoms or tassels.

Using same colors, make 2 braids to desired length.

Sew a pompom or tassel to end of each braid.

Thread other end of each braid through top of stocking just below cuff. Knot to secure. ●

COLOR KEY
☐ Color A of choice
▨ Color B of choice

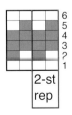

2-st rep

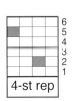

4-st rep

SOCK CHART A   **SOCK CHART B**

Little Mitten Garland

Knit a pretty little mitten collection to adorn your tree, your mantel or anyplace you need a touch of whimsy!

Design by Marji LaFreniere

Skill Level

 INTERMEDIATE

Finished Measurements

Mitten: 2 inches wide x 3½ inches long

Materials

- Brown Sheep Lamb's Pride Worsted (worsted weight; 85% wool/15% mohair; 190 yds/ 4 oz per skein): Approx 20–25 yds per mitten in colors of choice
- Fingering weight yarn (or needlepoint yarn or embroidery floss) assorted colors for embellishment
- Size 9 (5.5mm) double-point needles (set of 4) or size needed to obtain gauge
- Stitch marker
- Medium-size crochet hook (for chain): sizes F/5 (3.75mm)–J/10 (6mm) acceptable
- Wool wash

4 MEDIUM

Gauge

18 sts and 24 rnds = 4 inches/10cm in St st.

To save time, take time to check gauge.

Mitten

Note: *Make as many mittens as desired for garland.*

Body

Using color of choice, cast on 18 sts and distribute to 3 dpns. Mark beg of rnd and join, being careful not to twist.

Purl 1 rnd.

Knit 4 rnds.

Purl 1 rnd.

Knit 5 rnds.

Thumb opening rnd: K1; k3 with waste yarn, then slip those sts back to LH needle (these will be the thumb sts); reknit the 3 sts with working yarn, knit to end of rnd.

Knit 7 rnds.

Dec rnd: [K2tog] 9 times around—9 sts.

Knit 1 rnd.

Last rnd: [K2tog] 4 times, k1—5 sts.

Cut yarn, leaving a 5-inch tail.

Using tapestry needle, thread tail through rem sts, and pull tight.

Thumb

Pick out waste yarn from 3 thumb sts and transfer 5 live sts to dpns.

Join yarn; knit around, picking up 1 st on each side of thumb to close gaps—7 sts.

Knit 5 rnds.

Last rnd: [K2tog] 3 times, k1.

Cut yarn, leaving a 5-inch tail.

Using tapestry needle, thread tail through rem sts and pull tight.

Finishing
Weave in all ends.

Lightly hand-felt in warm water and wool wash. Let dry.

Embellishment
Note: *Refer to photos for sample embroidery.*

Using 1-yd strands of fingering weight yarn (or embroidery floss or needlepoint yarn) in 2 colors of choice, embroider patterns as desired on cuffs between purl rnds. Beg and end at side edge opposite thumb, leaving 6-inch tails for hangers. When embroidery is complete, braid tails, then knot end of braid, leaving a small tassel at end.

Garland Cord
Using color of choice and crochet hook, make a chain as long as desired. Cut yarn and fasten off. Weave in end.

Either thread chain through mittens or tie mittens to chain, as desired. ●

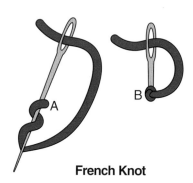

French Knot

It's in the Bag

Personalize your tree with this precious mini knitting bag complete with balls of yarn and needles!

Design by Lena Skvagerson for Annie's Signature Designs

Skill Level

 INTERMEDIATE

Finished Measurements

Approx 2¾ inches wide x 1½ inches tall (excluding handle)

Materials

- Fingering weight yarn: Small amount each 2 solid colors A and B
- Approx 1 yd each of different yarns (for mini balls)
- Size 2 (2.75mm) knitting needles or size needed to obtain gauge
- 2 bamboo marking pins (for mini needles)

1 SUPER FINE

Gauge

32 sts and 42 rnds = 4 inches/10cm in St st.

Exact gauge is not critical for this project.

Special Technique

4-St I-Cord: Cast on 4 sts; do not turn. *Slip sts back to LH needle, k4, do not turn; rep from * until cord is desired length. Bind off.

Knitting Bag

With A, cast on 20 sts.

Row 1 (WS): Knit.

Row 2 (eyelet row, RS): *K2tog, yo; rep from * to last 2 sts, k2.

Row 3: Knit.

Rows 4–26: Work in St st, beg and ending with a knit row.

Row 27: Knit.

Row 28 (eyelet row): *K2tog, yo; rep from * to last 2 sts, k2.

Row 29: Knit.

Bind off.

Finishing

Fold piece in half with cast-on and bound-off edges at top.

Sew side seams.

Handle

With A, work 4-St I-Cord until piece measures approx 4½ inches.

Bind off.

Sew ends of I-Cord to each side seam.

Cut 40-inch strand of B. Fold in half and secure folded end to a stationary object. Twist yarn until it begins to double back on itself. Fold in half again with both ends tog and allow to twist on itself. Thread cord through eyelet rows and tie a bow.

Make mini balls with leftover yarns; put balls in bag.

Insert 2 bamboo marking pins in bag for mini needles. ●

Littlest Matryoshka Doll

Here's a cheerful little trinket for your tree!

Design by Marji LaFreniere

Skill Level

◼◼◼◻ INTERMEDIATE

Finished Measurements

Circumference: Approx 5½–6 inches
Height: Approx 3½–4 inches

Materials

- DK or light worsted weight yarn: Approx 12 yds in 2 colors of choice (A and B)
- Fingering weight yarn, embroidery floss or needlepoint yarn: Small amounts various colors for embroidery
- Roving: very small amount each cream and black for needle-felting; pink (optional)
- Size 3 (3.25mm) double-point needles (set of 4) or size needed to obtain gauge
- Needle-felting needle
- Fiberfill
- Pink marker (optional)

Gauge

24 sts and 32 rnds = 4 inches/10cm in St st.

Exact gauge is not critical for this project.

Special Abbreviation

Make 1 (M1): Insert LH needle from front to back under horizontal strand between last st worked and next st on LH needle; knit through back of resulting loop.

Pattern Note

Doll is worked in the round from the bottom up.

Doll

Base

With A, cast on 12 sts and distribute to 3 dpns. Mark beg of rnd and join, being careful not to twist.

Rnd 1 and all odd-numbered rnds: Knit.

Rnd 2: K1, [M1, k2] 5 times, M1, k1—18 sts.

Rnd 4: K1, [M1, k3] 5 times, M1, k2—24 sts.

Rnd 6: K1, [M1, k4] 5 times, M1, k3—30 sts.

Rnds 8, 10, 12, 14 and 16: Knit.

Rnd 18: K5, [k2tog, k8] 3 times, k3—27 sts.

Rnd 20: [K2tog, k7] 3 times—24 sts.

Rnd 21: Knit. Cut A.

Top

With B, knit 8 rnds.

Turn piece inside out and weave in ends, using cast-on tail to tighten up the bottom before weaving in.

Dec rnd: [K2, k2tog] 6 times—18 sts.

Knit 1 rnd.

Last rnd: [K2tog, k1] 6 times—12 sts.

Cut yarn, leaving a 12-inch tail; thread tail through rem sts, but do not tighten up.

Finishing

Stuff doll fairly firmly with fiberfill but not so much as to make doll misshapen.

Pull tail closed and tighten securely, knotting end if desired for extra security. Weave in end.

Needle Felting

Note: Refer to photo as guide.

Face: Needle-felt a small amount of cream roving directly onto the doll where the face should be. Leave the edges for last and then use the felting needle to neaten them up and sort of "tuck" them under.

Hair: Using a very small amount of black roving, needle-felt hair to top of face.

Eyes: Roll almost microscopic little balls of black roving between your fingers, and then needle-felt them to face.

Cheeks: Color small pink cheeks using marker or blush. Optional: Needle-felt with pink roving.

Embroidery

Using fingering-weight yarn (or embroidery floss or needlepoint yarn) in various colors, embroider little flowers and spots on doll's "skirt" as desired, using lazy daisy stitches, French knots, etc., referring to photo.

Twisted-Cord Hanger

Cut 30-inch strand of yarn. Fold in half and secure folded end to a stationary object. Twist yarn until it begins to double back on itself. Fold in half again with both ends tog and allow to twist on itself. Thread cord through top of head. Tie ends tog in a knot; trim ends close to knot. Rotate cord so that knot is inside head. ●

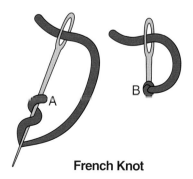

French Knot

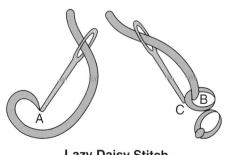

Lazy Daisy Stitch

Agnes the Christmas Lamb

This whimsical lamb is made in the round—body first, then ears and tail. Legs are added last to bring Agnes to life.

Design by Jodi Lewanda

Skill Level

■■■□ INTERMEDIATE

Finished Measurements

Height: 3½ inches

Length: 5 inches

Materials
- Textured bulky weight yarn: 20 yds white (A)
- DK weight yarn: 20 yds each white (B) and black (C)
- Size 2 (2.75mm) double-point needles (set of 4)
- Size 5 (3.75mm) double-point needles (set of 4) or size needed to obtain gauge
- Stitch marker
- Fiberfill

5 BULKY

3 LIGHT

Gauge

11 sts and 16 rnds = 4 inches/10cm in St st with larger dpns and A.

28 sts and 32 rnds = 4 inches/10cm in St st with smaller dpns and B and C.

Exact gauge is not critical for this project.

Special Technique

6-St I-Cord: With dpns, cast on 6 sts. *Do not turn, slide sts to other end of dpn, pull yarn taut across back, k6; rep from * until cord is desired length. Bind off.

Lamb

Body

With larger dpns and A, cast on 13 sts, then distribute to 3 dpns; pm for beg of rnd and join, being careful not to twist sts.

Note: *Leave room inside "circle" of cast-on sts to insert stuffing.*

Rnd 1: Kfb in each st around—26 sts.

Rnds 2–15: Knit.

Rnd 16: K2tog around—13 sts.

Cut A, leaving an 8-inch tail. Using tapestry needle, thread tail through rem sts, and pull tight.

Head

With larger dpns and A, cast on 10 sts, then distribute to 3 dpns; pm for beg of rnd and join, being careful not to twist sts.

Note: *Leave room inside "circle" of cast-on sts to insert stuffing.*

Rnd 1: Kfb in each st around—20 sts.

Rnds 2 and 3: Knit. Cut A.

Change to smaller dpns.

Rnd 4: With B, *kfb, k1; rep from * around—30 sts.

Rnds 5–10: Knit. Cut B.

Rnd 11: With C, [k2tog, k3] 6 times—24 sts.

Rnd 12: Knit.

Rnd 13: [K2tog, k2] 6 times—18 sts.

Rnd 14: [K2tog, k1] 6 times—12 sts.

Rnd 15: Knit.

Rnd 16: [K2tog, k1] 4 times—8 sts.

Rnd 17: K2tog around—4 sts.

Cut C, leaving an 8-inch tail.

Using tapestry needle, thread tail through rem sts, and pull tight.

Weave in all ends.

Embroidery & Stuffing

With C, embroider eyes with French knots referring to photo.

Stuff head.

Stuff body to desired fullness through cast-on "circle." Sew cast-on circle closed.

Position head onto body and using B, sew in place.

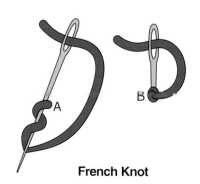

French Knot

Ear
Make 2

With smaller dpns and B, cast on 4 sts.

Knit 6 rows.

Next row: Ssk, k2tog—2 sts.

Bind off.

Tail

With smaller dpns and B, cast on 4 sts.

Knit 6 rows.

Next row: Ssk, k2tog—2 sts.

Next row: K2tog—1 st.

Fasten off.

Leg
Make 4

With smaller dpns and C, work 3 rnds of 6-St I-Cord; cut C.

With B, work 8 rnds of I-Cord.

Bind off.

Finishing

Position ears on side of head and sew in place.

Position tail on back end of body and sew in place.

Position legs on bottom of sheep and stitch in place.

Cut a 12-inch strand of B and make a loop; fasten it onto sheep's back for hanger.

Weave in ends. ●

Knitting Basics

Long-Tail Cast-On

Make a slip knot on the right needle.

Place the thumb and index finger of your left hand between the yarn ends with the long yarn end over your thumb, and the strand from the yarn ball over your index finger. Close your other fingers over the strands to hold them against your palm. Spread your thumb and index fingers apart and draw the yarn into a V.

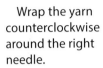

Place the needle in front of the strand around your thumb and bring it underneath this strand. Carry the needle over and under the strand on your index finger.

Draw the strand through the loop on your thumb. Drop the loop from your thumb and draw up the strand to form a stitch on the knitting needle.

Repeat until you have cast on the number of stitches indicated in the pattern.

Knit (k)

With yarn in back, insert the right needle from front to back into the next stitch on the left needle.

Bring the yarn under and over the right needle, wrapping the yarn counterclockwise around the needle.

Use the right needle to pull the loop through the stitch.

Slide the stitch off the left needle.

Purl (p)

With yarn in front, insert the right needle from back to front into the next stitch on the left needle.

Wrap the yarn counterclockwise around the right needle.

Use the right needle to pull the loop through the stitch and to the back.

Slide the stitch off left needle.

Bind Off

Binding Off (knit)

Knit the first two stitches on the left needle. Insert the left needle into the first stitch worked on the right needle, then lift that first stitch over the second stitch and off the right needle. Knit the next stitch and repeat.

When one stitch remains on the right needle, cut the yarn and draw the tail through the last stitch to fasten off.

Binding Off (purl)

Purl the first two stitches on the left needle.

Insert the left needle into the first stitch worked on the right needle, then lift the first stitch over the second stitch and off the right needle. Purl the next stitch and repeat.

When one stitch remains on the right needle, cut the yarn and draw the tail through the last stitch to fasten off.

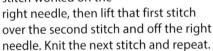
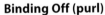

Increase (inc)

Bar Increase (knit: kfb)

Knit the next stitch but do not remove the original stitch from the left needle.

Insert the right needle behind the left needle and knit into the back of the same stitch.

Slip the original stitch off the left needle.

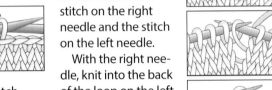

Bar Increase (purl: pfb)

Purl the next stitch but do not remove the original stitch from the left needle.

Insert the right needle behind the left needle and purl into the back of the same stitch.

Slip the original stitch off the left needle.

Make 1 With Left Twist (M1L)

Insert the left needle from front to back under the strand that runs between the stitch on the right needle and the stitch on the left needle.

With the right needle, knit into the back of the loop on the left needle.

To make this increase on the purl side, insert left needle in same manner and purl into the back of the loop.

Make 1 With Right Twist (M1R)

Insert the left needle from back to front under the strand that runs between the stitch on the right needle and the stitch on the left needle.

With the right needle, knit into the front of the loop on the left needle.

To make this increase on the purl side, insert left needle in same manner and purl into the front of the loop.

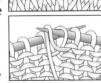

Make 1 With Backward Loop

Use your thumb to make a backward loop of yarn over the right needle. Slip the loop from your thumb onto the needle and pull to tighten.

Decrease (dec)

Knit 2 Together (k2tog)
Insert the right needle through the next two stitches on the left needle as if to knit. Knit these two stitches together as one.

Purl 2 Together (p2tog)
Insert the right needle through the next two stitches on the left needle as if to purl. Purl these two stitches together as one.

Slip, Slip, Knit (ssk)
Slip the next two stitches, one at a time, from the left needle to the right needle as if to knit.

Insert the left needle through both slipped stitches in front of the right needle.

Knit these two stitches together.

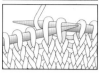

Slip, Slip, Purl (ssp)
Slip the next two stitches, one at a time, from the left needle to the right needle as if to knit.

Slip these stitches back to the left needle keeping them twisted.

Purl these two stitches together through their back loops.

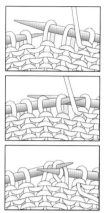

Standard Abbreviations

[ ] work instructions within brackets as many times as directed

( ) work instructions within parentheses in the place directed

** repeat instructions following the asterisks as directed

* repeat instructions following the single asterisk as directed

" inch(es)

approx approximately

beg begin/begins/beginning

CC contrasting color

ch chain stitch

cm centimeter(s)

cn cable needle

dec(s) decrease/decreases/decreasing

dpn(s) double-point needle(s)

g gram(s)

inc(s) increase/increases/increasing

k knit

k2tog knit 2 stitches together

kfb knit in front and back

kwise knitwise

LH left hand

m meter(s)

MC main color

mm millimeter(s)

oz ounce(s)

p purl

p2tog purl 2 stitches together

pat(s) pattern(s)

pm place marker

psso pass slipped stitch over

pwise purlwise

rem remain/remains/remaining

rep(s) repeat(s)

rev St st reverse stockinette stitch

RH right hand

rnd(s) rounds

RS right side

skp slip 1 knitwise, knit 1, pass slipped stitch over—a left-leaning decrease

sk2p slip 1 knitwise, knit 2 together, pass slipped stitch over the stitch from the knit-2-together decrease—a left-leaning double decrease

sl slip

sl 1 kwise slip 1 knitwise

sl 1 pwise slip 1 purlwise

sl st(s) slipped stitch(es)

ssk slip 2 stitches, 1 at a time, knitwise; knit these stitches together through the back loops—a left-leaning decrease

st(s) stitch(es)

St st stockinette stitch

tbl through back loop(s)

tog together

WS wrong side

wyib with yarn in back

wyif with yarn in front

yd(s) yard(s)

yfwd yarn forward

yo (yo's) yarn over(s)

Standard Yarn Weight System
Categories of yarn, gauge ranges and recommended needle sizes.

Yarn Weight Symbol & Category Names	0 LACE	1 SUPER FINE	2 FINE	3 LIGHT	4 MEDIUM	5 BULKY	6 SUPER BULKY	7 JUMBO
Type of Yarns in Category	Lace, Fingering, 10-Count Crochet Thread	Sock, Fingering, Baby	Sport, Baby	DK, Light Worsted	Worsted, Afghan, Aran	Chunky, Craft, Rug	Super Chunky, Roving	Roving
Knit Gauge Range* in Stockinette Stitch to 4 inches	33–40 sts**	27–32 sts	23–26 sts	21–24 sts	16–20 sts	12–15 sts	7–11 sts	6 sts and fewer
Recommended Needle in Metric Size Range	1.5–2.25mm	2.25–3.25mm	3.25–3.75mm	3.75–4.5mm	4.5–5.5mm	5.5–8mm	8–12.75mm	12.75mm and larger
Recommended Needle U.S. Size Range	000 to 1	1 to 3	3 to 5	5 to 7	7 to 9	9 to 11	11 to 17	17 and larger

* GUIDELINES ONLY: The above reflect the most commonly used gauges and needle sizes for specific yarn categories.
** Lace weight yarns are often knitted on larger needles and hooks to create lacy, openwork patterns. Accordingly, a gauge range is difficult to determine. Always follow the gauge stated in your pattern.

Skill Levels

BEGINNER
Beginner projects for first-time knitters using basic stitches. Minimal shaping.

EASY
Easy projects using basic stitches, repetitive stitch patterns, simple color changes, and simple shaping and finishing.

INTERMEDIATE
Intermediate projects with a variety of stitches, mid-level shaping and finishing.

EXPERIENCED
Experienced projects using advanced techniques and stitches, detailed shaping and refined finishing.

Deck the Halls is published by Annie's, 306 East Parr Road, Berne, IN 46711. Printed in USA. Copyright © 2015, 2017 Annie's. All rights reserved. This publication may not be reproduced in part or in whole without written permission from the publisher.

RETAIL STORES: If you would like to carry this publication or any other Annie's publication, visit AnniesWSL.com.

Every effort has been made to ensure that the instructions in this publication are complete and accurate. We cannot, however, take responsibility for human error, typographical mistakes or variations in individual work. Please visit AnniesCustomerService.com to check for pattern updates.

ISBN: 978-1-57367-693-9

8 9 10 11 12 13 14